W9-BQT-672

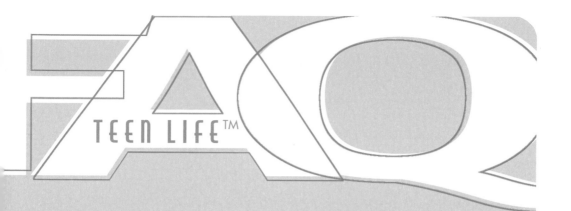

TEEN LIFE™

FREQUENTLY ASKED QUESTIONS ABOUT

Being Part of a Military Family

Joyce Hart

ROSEN
PUBLISHING®
New York

To all the friends made along the military family journey

Published in 2010 by The Rosen Publishing Group, Inc.
29 East 21st Street, New York, NY 10010

Library of Congress Cataloging-in-Publication Data

Hart, Joyce, 1954–
Frequently asked questions about being part of a military family / Joyce Hart.—1st ed.
    p. cm.—(FAQ: teen life)
Includes bibliographical references and index.
ISBN-13: 978-1-4358-5328-7 (library binding)
1. Children of military personnel—United States—Juvenile literature.
2. Families of military personnel—United States—Juvenile literature.
3. United States—Armed Forces—Military life—Juvenile literature.
4. Children of military personnel—United States—Life skills guides.
5. Families of military personnel—United States—Life skills guides.
I. Title.
UB403.H37 2010
355.1'20973—dc22

2008055612

Manufactured in the United States of America

3 1967 01114 4790

Contents

WHAT DOES IT MEAN TO BE PART OF A MILITARY FAMILY?

Being part of a military family can be both one of the most exciting times of your life as well as one of the most stressful. You are probably very proud of your military parent, whether this is your father or your mother or, in some cases, both your parents. Yet you also have to deal with your parent being gone for long periods of time while worrying about his or her welfare.

However, being a part of a military family also gives you the chance to travel to places you might never have visited and meet people who may never have entered your life otherwise. Your family could be sent anywhere from Hawaii to Florida to California and anywhere in between. You might even get the chance to live in Bermuda or Germany or Japan. Of course, the trauma of moving and saying good-bye to your friends can be difficult, but then you will also have

Families gather to send their military members away. Military families support one another because they share similar circumstances.

the chance of making new friends while developing a strong and sustaining correspondence with your old gang.

Forging Bonds

Moving from one place to another can also bring your family closer together. As you pack up your things and either drive or fly to your new home, there is security in having your family around you. You and your brothers and sisters share the same challenges of entering a new school and making new friends.

These shared experiences help to tighten bonds and strengthen supportive relationships with your siblings.

Another group of people who will help you are the other military families who completely understand and share in what you are going through. Teenagers whose parents are enlisted in the military know how hard it can be to move and start all over again. They know how tough it can be to have a parent who must leave the family behind. But they can also share stories with you about their experiences, and together you can learn ways to cope with the hardships. By sharing your experiences, you begin to build a community around you, a community of friends who understand your feelings, sometimes even before you open up and share them.

Being part of a military family will leave its mark on you, even into your adult years. As you grow older, the memory of tough times will probably fade away, but the great and enriching times will remain more closely held and cherished. You will have friends all over the nation and maybe all over the world. You will have met people from different cultures, or at least from different places and backgrounds. You will have seen places in person you might otherwise have visited only in books, movies, or online. When you are old enough, you might even decide that you, too, want to enlist and have a military career—and military family—of your own.

The Big Military Family

So you find yourself part of a military family. Though the resulting changes in your life could be making you feel both proud

Every year, thousands of men and women join one of the four branches of the U.S. armed forces to help protect the country. They pick the U.S. Army, Navy, Air Force, or Marines.

and a little stressed, it might make you feel better to know that you are not alone. Millions of families in the United States feature one or even two parents who are members of the U.S. armed forces.

The United States relies on these soldiers for protection. U.S. military forces are trained to respond to attacks on this country, to defend U.S. interests abroad, and to act as peacekeepers in other countries. In 2008, almost 1.5 million men and women volunteered to work for the military by joining one of the four major armed forces. These armed forces are the U.S. Army, the U.S. Air Force, the U.S. Navy, and the U.S. Marine Corps.

Who Is in Charge of the Military?

The president of the United States is called the commander in chief of all the U.S. military forces. This means that he is the person who makes the final decisions about how the military forces are to be used. However, the president appoints a person to work as the secretary of defense to help in making those decisions. The secretary of defense also makes sure that the men and women in the military are prepared to go wherever they are needed. The Department of Defense is where the secretary works.

The Department of Defense, which is located in the Pentagon building outside of Washington, D.C., is responsible for supplying all the armed forces that are needed to protect the United States. The secretary of defense, along with the top military officers and leaders in the U.S. military forces, often meet at the Pentagon. These people discuss where soldiers are needed to keep peace in the world and protect American security interests. Then the secretary of defense advises the president and suggests the best ways to do this.

What Are the Different Branches of Military Service?

U.S. Army: The U.S. Army is the oldest branch of the U.S. military forces. It was founded in 1775, just prior to the declaration of independence from Great Britain. Today, there are about 500,000 soldiers in the U.S. Army. These soldiers (and sometimes their families) live not only in the United States but also in Asia,

Not all people who serve in the military are shipped overseas. Here, an Army National Guard soldier helps a victim of Hurricane Katrina in New Orleans, Louisiana.

Europe, and the Middle East. Regular army soldiers work for the military full-time. They hold no other job outside the military.

The Army Reserve is part of the U.S. Army. Unlike regular army soldiers, reserve soldiers, after they have gone through training, return to their regular lives, working as teachers, bankers, construction workers, and other civilian (nonmilitary) jobs until they are needed. During peacetime, reserve soldiers normally have to leave their families only for a couple of weeks each year for training exercises.

The Army National Guard is another section of the U.S. Army. Just like the Army Reserve, the Army National Guard is made up of what are called citizen-soldiers. They spend some time in training, but they keep their regular jobs and live at home except when they are needed. Army National Guard soldiers are mostly used in times of disasters and crisis inside the United States. When Hurricane Katrina caused so much devastation and chaos in New Orleans in 2005, the secretary of defense called up the Army National Guard. It helped the police force in Louisiana maintain order, restore calm, and help the state's citizens reach safety and obtain food and shelter.

U.S. Marine Corps: Like the U.S. Army, the U.S. Marine Corps was also founded in 1775. The Marine Corps is the smallest branch of the U.S. military forces. There are fewer than 200,000 marines. Marines are stationed around the world, always ready to fight for peace as soon as they are needed. In fact, the marines are often the first soldiers to arrive in a war zone. As with the army, the marines also have a reserve section. The U.S. Marine Reserves, however, differ from that of the army. In order to be a member of the U.S. Marine Reserves, men and women must have first served at least four years of regular (full-time) duty as a regular marine.

U.S. Navy: President George Washington, in 1775, established the U.S. Navy to help fight against the British, as well as to stop pirates who were attacking the shores of the early colonies. Over the years, the U.S. Navy has grown, and today there are more than 300,000 men and women enlisted in the service. The

It takes courage and commitment to become a member of the armed forces. Soldiers go through difficult, frightening, and dangerous training, such as parachute jumping, to prepare them for future assignments.

main job of the U.S. Navy is to protect the waters around the United States and vital shipping channels around the world. The U.S. Navy also has a reserve branch.

U.S. Air Force: The U.S. Air Force is the youngest branch of the military forces. In 1920, army soldiers were first trained to fly. As their numbers grew, these pilots were said to be in the U.S. Army/Air Corps. It wasn't until 1947, after World War II, that the U.S. Air Force became a separate military branch.

Today, there are more than 350,000 members of the U.S. Air Force. These military people protect the United States by patrolling American airspace and backing up U.S. ground forces in times of war. U.S. Air Force pilots are often equipped with weapons and instruments that allow them to attack—or gather vital information about—the enemy from their vantage point high above the land. The U.S. Air Force also flies troops, military equipment, and supplies to wherever the military needs them.

chapter
two

HOW DO I COPE WITH MOVING AWAY?

Life in a military family is in some ways the same as life in any family. Military families share meals together, go on vacations, and visit grandparents just as any ordinary family might. However, life in a military family is also very different from life in a civilian family in which the parents have jobs in a bank, a school, an office, or a hospital. One of the biggest differences between the lives of a civilian family and a family that is involved in one of the military branches is that a military family is often transferred from one place to another.

How Often Will You Move?

There is one certainty about living in a military family: you will have to get used to moving. The number of times

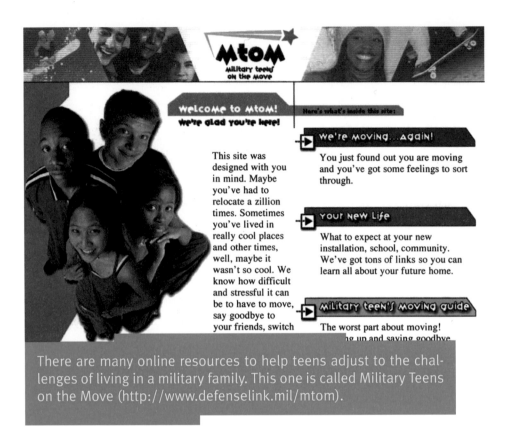

There are many online resources to help teens adjust to the challenges of living in a military family. This one is called Military Teens on the Move (http://www.defenselink.mil/mtom).

you will move is uncertain. Some soldiers and their families move every two years. Some move more. Others move less often. But all military families will experience at least one move, and moving can be challenging, especially for school-age children.

There are a lot of different ways to look at moving. Going to live in a new location can be very exciting. You might move from the Midwest, for example, to the Pacific Coast. This will give you a chance to see the ocean for the first time in your life. Or you could move from Florida to Alaska and experience summer days in which the sun never completely sets, since parts of Alaska experience almost twenty-four hours of sunshine during the summer season.

A lot of military families are stationed overseas. This means you could move from the United States to Germany or Japan. You could live in an entirely different culture in which people speak a different language, drive on the left side (instead of the right side) of the road, and eat food that you have never tasted. These experiences can provide you with a whole new way of looking at the world and expose you to knowledge and experiences that American teens back home don't have access to.

Of course, there are some things about moving that are not as much fun and are therefore harder to do. But just because moving might be challenging does not mean that it is impossible to do or should be avoided. Change is difficult, but it can also be very exciting, allowing you to mature emotionally, intellectually, socially, and experientially.

Where Will You Live?

There are usually two options for military families who are transferred to new locations. Most military bases provide family housing on the bases themselves. If housing is not provided on a military base, or if families want to live somewhere else, the military gives families a special housing allowance. This allows them to afford houses in the residential communities that are outside the base but still nearby.

Last year, the Department of Defense spent $20 billion to renovate older houses or build new ones on military bases around the world. If your family decides to live in military housing, your new home will probably look similar to most typical suburban houses or apartment complexes. Living on a base means that your military parent will be able to commute more easily between his or her job and home. You will live among families who have a lot in common. All the children in your new military community will know what it is like to have a soldier parent. They will also all know what it feels like to have to move a lot. And chances are you will all go to the same school.

Living in military housing in a foreign country also provides the added benefit of going to an on-base school in which English is the language of instruction. You will be among teens who all come from the same country and speak the same language, making it that much easier to adjust to suddenly being in a new home, surrounded by new people, in a new country and an entirely new and different culture. Most military bases provide certain amenities for the children of servicemen and women, such as a teen center and other places and activities in which teens can gather, get acquainted, and socialize. Living on a military base often allows you to develop long-lasting relationships. Sometimes units, or groups, of soldiers are transferred together, which means that the friends you make on one base might end up moving with you to the next base.

Not all families choose to live on a military base, however. Some prefer to live within the civilian community, whether that community is located in the United States or in another country. Living off base provides a greater variety of schools to select from. The city or town also often offers a wider selection of activities, entertainment, shopping, and culture. By living off base, you mingle with the local people who have lived in the area most of their lives. You can learn more about the local culture this way.

Saying Good-Bye

Outside of your family, friends offer you a lot of support. You turn to your friends to help you through difficult times that you are less comfortable sharing with your parents or siblings. Your friends can cheer you up when you are feeling down. They make you feel good about yourself. Getting to the point where you feel comfortable with people your own age can take a long time. You might have known some of your friends since you were in first grade. So leaving them can be sad and even scary. How will you ever replace them?

Well, the truth is that you will never replace them, nor should you try to. They are special and can't be replaced. They also don't have to be discarded just because you're moving. For your own sake, you will have to make new friends, but your old friends will always be some of the best people you'll ever know. Saying good-bye to them might be the hardest thing you'll ever do. But the trick is to do it with gusto.

Throw your friends a party. Invite them all. Feed them, talk to them, hug them. Let them know how much you have appreciated them through the years. Pull out old photographs if you have them. Reminisce about the details of how you met them and some of the special times you shared. Tell them how you will remember them. Then take a lot of photographs and send

Leaving friends behind is one of the most difficult challenges military families face. Be sure to honor and celebrate your friendships before you leave, and work hard to maintain them long-distance.

them to your friends later, so you will all remember this special party and the strong bonds of memory, experience, and feelings you share.

Or, instead of throwing a party, you might want to share an outing together and create new memories to cherish. Go to the beach together, or maybe you could go to the mountains and take a long hike. Get on the subway or bus with a group of your friends and go to a different part of the city that you have never visited. You might also go shopping, go see a movie, or just hit your favorite hangout. The key is to do something together and share your memories and your feelings for one another before you have to say good-bye. And this doesn't mean that you have to get all mushy and sentimental if you don't feel comfortable with that. The point is to have fun and focus on how much these friends mean to you.

Remember, too, to say good-bye to your town. This might sound like a strange thing to do, but this town has played a role in your life. You have a long-term relationship with it. Get on your bike or on a bus and visit some of your favorite places in town. Let each place stir the memories you have collected. Can you remember when you first came to this town? Or if this is your hometown, go visit your elementary school and remember what you felt like on your first day of school. Is there a community center or an athletic field where you have spent a lot of time? What about a favorite beach or park? Make sure you take lots of photographs. In those moments when you miss this town, after you've left, photographs can be a good substitute for being there in person.

Staying in Touch

Today, more than at any other time in history, staying in touch with your friends is very easy to do. Not too long ago, the only way of communicating with a friend left behind was to write a letter and send it as "snail mail" through the U.S. Postal Service. Or you might have made a long-distance telephone call, which back then was a lot more expensive than it is today and meant you could speak only for a few minutes, usually late at night.

Thanks to the Internet, it is easier today than at any other time to stay in touch with friends. E-mail, instant messaging, webcams, photo and video sharing, and blogs can help keep connections strong.

But now, you have so many options that you have no excuse not to keep in touch—from text messaging, e-mail, chat rooms, social networking sites, blogs, and posted home videos, to setting up a webcam on your computer so that you can not only talk but see one another at the same time. Your choices are wide and diverse. Communications are so instantaneous today that it may barely feel like you have moved away. Yes, it will not be the same as going to classes together or hanging out after school, but it's the next best thing.

Even though you are changing, if you stay in touch with your old friends, you can keep those friends for life. You will have plenty of occasions in the years ahead to get together with old friends and remember everything you have shared. The key word is "sharing." Whether you share the details of your lives in person, online, or on the phone, the more things you know about one another, the deeper the friendship will grow, no matter how many miles separate you.

Looking Forward

Let's say that your parent has received military orders to move to another town on the other side of the state, or to another state on the other side of the country, or to another country on the other side of the world. How are you going to prepare yourself for this change?

The best way to dispel your fear of the unknown is to gain knowledge about and familiarity with your new home. Whether you have a computer at home or you have to go to the library to use one, you can go online and find a lot of information about your new town. You are sure to find Web pages about the town's schools, geography, history, current events, people, entertainment, shopping, and attractions. Just write the name of the town and the state or the country in which it is located, and take a virtual tour of all that the town has to offer. You might not receive a complete picture of your new town, but you will discover photographs of special places, a history of the town, the weather you might expect in any given season, and the name of the school you might attend. In many places, the schools have their own individual Web sites that you can visit.

There will still be a lot more to discover, and you'll just have to wait until you get there to really begin exploring. However, the Internet can provide you with enough advance information to make you feel more comfortable about moving there. You can even use Internet maps and satellite pictures to pinpoint exactly where your new school and new house are located. Some school Web sites provide names of teens you can e-mail to ask more specific questions, such as what they think of the school, who their favorite teachers are, and what are some of the local spots that are the most fun. If you know the neighborhood you'll be living in, you might even find out if there are any teens living close to your new home who go to the same school you will be attending.

The best advice about looking forward to your next move is to keep your spirits up. Although leaving is hard, beginning to get involved in all the exciting things that are waiting for you in your new location is the most effective way to stay positive and make a smooth transition. In any challenge you face, your attitude plays a big part in ensuring that you will enjoy what lies ahead of you, be successful in your efforts, and attract people to you and your positive spirit.

WHAT ARE SOME STRATEGIES FOR ADJUSTING TO MY NEW SCHOOL AND COMMUNITY?

You are about to spend your first day at your new school. Being a new kid in school is very hard—you don't know anybody, nobody knows you, and they all know each other and have formed solid friendships before you arrived. Some people in these situations are very shy, while others are very outgoing and welcome the challenge of making new friends. But wherever you stand on the shyness spectrum, here are some tips on how you might adjust to your new environment.

Adapting to Your New School

For a teen, one of the most important adjustments to a new school will probably be making friends. The shy ones

Training for a sport not only helps you release tension but also offers you a chance to get in shape and meet new people. This exercise class is held on a military base and is for military families.

might stand off to the side and hope that someone will come up and start talking to them. Shy people feel too awkward to go up to a stranger and introduce themselves. The thought of being rejected or made fun of is just too painful.

Whether you are shy or not, you can meet people without barging into the center of a crowd and saying, "Hi. I'm the new person in town, and I would like to meet you." If you acted this boldly, you might find that everyone looks at each other with disbelief and walks away. However, there is another way of

introducing yourself to classmates without coming on too strong
and scaring them away.

Join a Sports Team

Back at your old school, you might have developed a special
athletic skill. Maybe you played as point guard on your basket-
ball team. Maybe you were on the cross-country or track team,
or you were on a winning doubles tennis team. There is also
the possibility that you loved to swim, although you never
joined a formal team because your school didn't have one. But
your new school does.

There's the chance that you might not even have known that
you had any athletic ability at all, but now that you're a little
older and a little stronger, you think you might really like to play
for the soccer team. So you hear about tryouts and decide to go
check out how good the other kids are. You watch them and
think that you can play at least as well as most of them, and even
a little better than a few. So you try out, too.

Whether you make the team or not, trying out for a sports team
will give you a shared experience with the group of teens that join
you. You might practice with them for a few weeks and even make
the first few cuts. In the process, you not only learn how good you
are and how much true interest you have in the sport, but you will
also learn some of the kids' names. You might find that a couple
live in your neighborhood. You might run into others in town. You
start learning more about them as they learn about you. Your peers
will see you no longer as just the "new kid." For them, you will

Joining an after-school club will help take your mind off the sadness of leaving your old school and your old friends behind. It will also introduce you to new people—and maybe some new friends—who share your interests.

now have a name, known interests, and an intriguing back-ground and history. These details that you are learning about each other are the building blocks of new friendships.

Join a Club

Maybe you have no interest in sports. That's OK, since there are other ways of mixing with a group of people with whom you share similar interests. You can join an after-school club.

Today, most schools offer a wide selection of clubs organized around specific interests. These range from academic clubs, which help students prepare for college, to military clubs, which help prepare students for eventual enlistment as soldiers. Journalism and foreign language clubs have long been popular, as have chess and science clubs. There are also clubs that focus on the arts, such as choir, orchestra, marching band, photography, painting, and dancing.

Clubs that are organized around the theme of culture and personal background include Asian American clubs, African American clubs, and clubs for students for whom English is a second language. There are also computer clubs, math clubs, and even clubs for students interested in manga and anime. Some schools have drama clubs and environmental clubs. Debate clubs are sometimes available to hone students' argumentation skills. Many schools also offer leadership skills training clubs, student government clubs, and business clubs.

You could also become a member of the school newspaper or the school yearbook. The idea is to find a group of students with

Fellow climbers encourage this new member of a climbing club and offer helpful advice. Sharing cooperative and supportive experiences like this helps deepen new relationships.

whom you have a common interest, then join in and have some fun outside of your classes. The experiences you share in these clubs will help you make new friends.

Recognizing and Relieving Stress

Stress is almost always present in people's lives, sometimes even without them knowing it. When a person is hungry, he might feel a minor form of stress that motivates him to find something to eat. Or when someone is crossing a busy street, she might hear a horn honking. The low-grade stress of that intrusive noise wakes her out of a daydream and makes her scurry out of the way of an oncoming car. Students might also feel stress when they see a boy or girl they've developed a crush on coming down the school hall toward them. Stress comes in many different forms and reaches many different levels of intensity.

WHAT ARE SOME STRATEGIES FOR ADJUSTING
TO MY NEW SCHOOL AND COMMUNITY?

29

Stress can work both for you and against you. Stress that makes you want to get better grades can motivate you to study harder. However, if that stress gets out of control, you can become so agitated by the heavy load of anxiety that you can't study at all. Becoming aware of stress and its symptoms can help you decide when you are experiencing a harmful amount and what to do to control it.

According to the Mayo Clinic, the following can be signs that you are experiencing too much stress. First there are physical symptoms, such as constant headaches, shortness of breath, clenched jaws, too many instances of upset stomach, fatigue, and problems sleeping. Then there are psychological symptoms, such as worrying too much; being irritable, angry, or sad too often; being forgetful; or feeling negative about everything around you. Symptoms that affect your behavior can include eating too much or completely losing your appetite, alcohol and substance abuse, being unable to keep up with schoolwork, and getting into frequent arguments with friends or family.

Moving often causes stress. Generally speaking, almost everyone encounters some stress when they must leave one familiar environment and move to a new and unfamiliar one. Saying good-bye to friends is difficult and sad. Packing up all your things, selling the house, and even traveling from one place to another can make your family feel edgy. There are a lot of unknown factors ahead of you, and not knowing what to expect can make you feel both excited and nervous.

Where you once had a very patient father, you might now see someone who barks out answers to your questions. Where you

Stress can drain you of energy. It is a good idea to make time just for yourself. Use it to relax, reflect, and clear your mind. Face your sadness, but also think about the positive things going on in your life.

once had a very laidback mother, you might now witness a mother who can't sleep and wears an angry scowl on her face at the breakfast table. Your brothers and sisters might fight more, and you might be ready to blow your top yourself. These are all signs of stress overload. But you don't have to become a victim of stress. There are ways to lessen your stress levels and manage, or even overcome, the anxiety.

According to the National Institute of Health, the first step toward diminishing the level of stress you are experiencing is to identify the source of your stress. Find a quiet place, relax as much as you can, and examine your thoughts. Try to identify what you are thinking about that is causing you so much worry. Is there anything that is making you feel sad, nervous, or angry? You might want to have some paper and a pen with you so that you can write down what you discover. When you're done, find someone you can talk to. It might surprise you to find that just talking with a friend or a mentor (a pastor, guidance counselor, therapist, teacher, parent, favorite aunt, or older sibling or cousin) about what is bothering you often releases a lot of the stress.

Once you pinpoint what is bothering you and have talked to someone about it, you still have some work to do. You will want to take some time each day to think about what is causing the stress. Try to visualize the thing that is stressful. Actually try to see it.

If the source of your stress is one of your teachers, try to see him or her in your mind. Then examine why that person causes you stress. Imagine what you might do to minimize the stress in your relationship with this person. Adjust your image of this person so that the stress level associated with him or her lessens. Ask yourself some questions: Is it really what this person is doing, or is it my attitude toward this person? How can I interact with this person from now on in a way that will be less stressful and more productive and positive? Then create a new visualization in which you and that person are having a relationship that has no stress associated with it. You can practice visualization in a lot of different ways. Just remember that the goal is to eventually create an image in which the stress is greatly reduced.

An older student living on a military base tutors a younger "military brat." The sense of community among military families who live both on and off base is strong. People look out for each other, and children and teens understand each other's lives, worries, and stresses really well.

Another way to diminish stress is through physical activity and caring for your body. For example, review your diet. Sugary foods and drinks are not good for your mind or body when you are stressed. Start eating healthier foods. Also, make sure you are getting enough sleep. Put yourself on a regular exercise plan. Stretching out your muscles is a good way to reduce stress. Alcohol, tobacco, and caffeine, contrary to some people's beliefs, do not help reduce stress and can actually make stress worse. They should be avoided, especially during periods of great stress, anxiety, and depression. Instead, become involved in the practice of tai chi, yoga, or meditation. These three activities help you become more conscious of your stress and its sources and then relieve and release it. Your local health club or YMCA probably offers classes in these activities.

chapter four

WHAT CAN I EXPECT WHEN MY MILITARY PARENT IS DEPLOYED?

In a time of war or national disaster, such as a hurricane or flood, there is a high chance that your military parent will be deployed. Even in peacetime, your parent might be deployed in order to gain special training or to take special classes. Deployment means that your military parent has received orders from the base commander to move from the home base to a new location. Deployment is different from a transfer. In a transfer, your whole family moves to a new location. In a deployment, only your military parent will be moved.

Sometimes, the deployment is for a short period of time, such as a few weeks or a month. Other times, the deployment period can last up to six months. During wartime, the deployment usually extends to a year or more. Often, when a parent receives deployment orders,

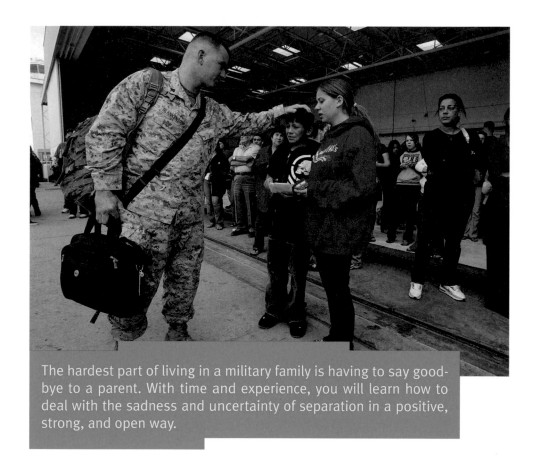

The hardest part of living in a military family is having to say good-bye to a parent. With time and experience, you will learn how to deal with the sadness and uncertainty of separation in a positive, strong, and open way.

it does not mean that he or she will be transferred immediately to a new location. However, the time between receiving deployment orders and the moment when your military parent must leave varies. It all depends on the situation. If your parent is being deployed because of an emergency, his or her leaving might happen quickly after receiving deployment orders. When the United States is involved in a war, the chances of your military parent being deployed are much higher than during peacetime.

Many schools, especially those on or near a military base, have special resources for students whose parents are deployed, such as this book on deployment and family separation.

Helping Your Family
After a Deployment Order

It is easy to feel like you have no control over the situation when your military parent receives deployment orders. You can't throw the deployment papers away and pretend that your parent won't have to leave. You also can't act as if the deployment won't affect you or your family. But this does not mean that you are helpless to do anything.

After receiving deployment orders, your military parent, as well as the rest of your family, must face the fact that things have changed. Your military parent will have to leave and may be gone for a long time. Depending on where your military parent is going and what your parent will be doing, there may be increased danger in his or her life. These are facts that cannot be denied. Facing the hard facts and your feelings about them is important.

Encourage your family to take time every night to sit down and talk about the emotions you are experiencing, individually and collectively. If you are feeling fearful, what is causing it? What are you afraid of? Are your brothers and sisters feeling the same fears? What about your parents? Are you sad? Are you angry? Sometimes, just talking about your emotions makes you feel better. Knowing that you are not the only one experiencing these emotions can make you feel less lonesome. It is also possible that something you are afraid of is based on rumors, rather than on true facts. Opening up to your family might lessen your fear and anxiety and clear up any misconceptions that are causing you needless extra worry.

Taking time to express your love for your parents not only offers an opportunity to deepen your relationship with them but can also make you feel stronger and more secure and supported.

Be sure to realize that some of the fear and anger you are feeling is because you love your parents. So don't be shy about letting them know how deep your love for them is. If you open up to your parents, your parents will be encouraged to open up to you as well. This mutual honesty will make everyone feel more loved and secure and optimistic.

According to information put out by the Department of Veteran Affairs, military families often go through several emotional stages after a soldier receives deployment orders. Depending on their age, children of military parents may react with a loss of appetite, anger as expressed through temper tantrums, an inability to sleep, and even a sense of guilt, believing that their parent is leaving because of something they did.

If you have younger siblings, you can help them by watching carefully for these signs of stress. You can help them feel less scared by talking to them and trying your best to show them through your own words and actions that you believe everything is going to be all right. You can do this by sticking to your studies, controlling your temper, and being helpful around the house. You might not be able to control where your military parent is going, how long he or she will be gone, or what he or she will have to face while away, but you can control yourself.

Face Your Own Emotions

If you are feeling anxiety, anger, fear, or any other strong emotion that can be destructive, don't fall into the trap of drugs or alcohol. Some teens believe that drugs and alcohol help ease the grip of their negative emotions, but this is not true. Drugs and alcohol often actually act as depressants, leaving you feeling lower than you did before you consumed them. You will eventually have to deal with your emotions anyway, but by the time you do, you might have an alcohol or drug problem to deal with, too.

If you become overwhelmed with your emotions, and your parents are too distracted with their own feelings to talk with you, seek out your guidance counselor at school, a teacher who makes you feel at ease, a family doctor, a coach, or a close friend whom you admire. The military also has lots of mental health resources and many on- and off-base therapists whom you can talk to (see the For More Information section of this book for some of these military health resources). Make an appointment with that person so that you have his or her undivided attention, and then just talk your heart out. Do this over a period of time because your feelings might not all come out on the first encounter. It's sometimes hard to open yourself up to another person. But if you choose the right person, opening up will make you feel strong enough to cope with whatever you are dealing with.

Staying in Touch with Your Military Parent

One of the nicest ways of staying in touch with your military parent while he or she is deployed is over the phone. Hearing your parent's voice is the best, most affirming reminder of how much you miss and love her or him. But phone calls may be rare, and they are often short, so the ability to exchange important news and information is reduced. Fortunately, you have other options.

Sending e-mails back and forth is one way to keep your communications alive. Even if your parent is unable to do this on a daily basis, that doesn't mean you can't provide this service for him or her. Short e-mail notes about how your day went, how your studies are progressing, and what new friends you've met can bring a smile to your parent's face. You can even upload and

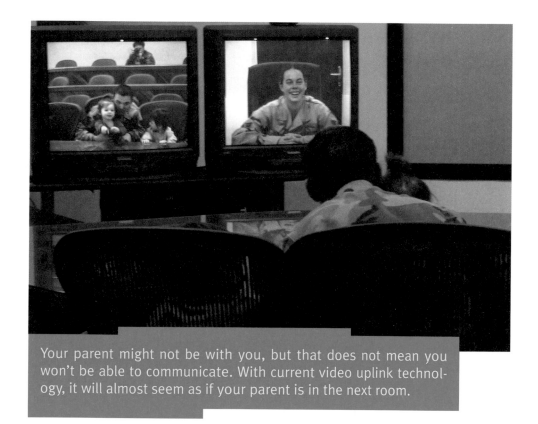

Your parent might not be with you, but that does not mean you won't be able to communicate. With current video uplink technology, it will almost seem as if your parent is in the next room.

send photos, write poems, copy jokes you found on the Internet, or just tell your parent that you love him or her. While it is important to share your emotional experiences with your military parent, try to be upbeat and positive when communicating with him or her. That will help both of you feel better.

Another way of communicating is to make a tape, either audio or video. Include your brothers and sisters, if you have them. You could just let everyone say whatever they want. You could create a comedy skit or a song and dance routine. Make up your own rap, letting your parent know how much you miss

Ten Great Questions to Ask a Military Family Counselor

1 How often will I be able to talk with my deployed parent on the phone?

2 How long is my parent's tour of duty?

3 Will my parent be granted any leaves of absence during the tour of duty and be able to visit us?

4 After my parent completes this tour of duty, how long will he or she be able to stay with us before being deployed again?

5 Why do military families have to be relocated, rather than remain at their original base?

Will I go to school on the base or within the civilian community?

How do I deal with classmates who are opposed to war and the military?

My mother is not doing well since my father was deployed. Where can I get help for her?

My grades are slipping since we moved. Can anyone help me catch up?

Since my father was deployed, my stomach has been hurting a lot and I haven't been sleeping well. Should I seek help?

him or her. Either send the tape in the mail or upload the audio or video file on your computer and e-mail it.

Reunion and Post-Deployment

Reunion with your returning parent will probably be a joyful celebration. But both your military parent and all the other members of your family may face some challenges after he or she returns home. Whether your military parent has been gone for six months or a year, important changes have occurred. Your military parent has had experiences that you and your family have not shared. And you and your family have had your own experiences that your military parent has not personally witnessed. Everyone has become a little older and, in some ways, has grown more independent.

It's important during this time to exercise as much patience with each other as you can. Don't expect your military parent to immediately fit into the schedules that have been created since he or she has been gone. In your military parent's absence, you may have taken on responsibilities that you did not have when he or she was last living with you. You might have taken on family duties, for instance, that your military parent used to do, such as mowing the lawn or cleaning the house. You may have gotten used to taking orders only from one parent, but now you have to listen to two. Your military parent, on the other hand, has been focused on taking care of his or her military duties and may no longer be used to being in a family situation and dealing with teens and children.

As families reunite, joy and relief often crowd out memories of sadness and stress. Family dynamics may have changed during the deployment, and family life may be awkward at first. But the important thing is that the family is together again and is loving and supporting each other during the transition and beyond.

Post-deployment is a time for readjustment. Although you have known your military parent all your life, in some ways, he or she might feel a little bit like a stranger right now. This may be especially true if your military parent is recuperating from a wound or is suffering from what is called post-traumatic stress disorder (PTSD), a psychological condition that results from enduring an extremely stressful and terrifying event or series of events.

There are resources listed in the back of this book that will help you understand some of the challenges that your family might face and what you can do to help. Just remember that after all the excitement of having your military parent returned to your home, you might still have some serious challenges ahead of you. Be patient and understanding. Help the other members of your family do the same by being a good example for them.

WHAT IF I AM THINKING ABOUT A CAREER IN THE MILITARY?

How should you go about considering a military career for yourself? Well, first you should do as much research as possible. Since you have a military parent, asking him or her about enlisting and life in the armed services would be a good place to start. Next, you might want to talk to a school counselor. You can also do research online. By researching the various branches of the military, you can learn the differences between enlisting and serving in the navy, army, air force, and marines. There are also Web sites that might inform you of what military life is like from a soldier's perspective.

You might also want to visit a military recruiting office, which will have up-to-date information about how much money you will receive, how long you will have to serve,

If you are thinking about joining the military, you can begin your training in school through a Reserve Officers' Training Corps (ROTC) program. Ask your school counselor how to join.

what your responsibilities will be, and what benefits are available. If your high school has a Reserve Officers' Training Corp (ROTC) program, make an appointment to talk to one of the program's instructors.

The Advantages and Disadvantages of Military Life

Besides knowing that you are doing your part in serving your country, especially in a time of need, there are many other

Navy recruits practice their skills in the protective environment of an indoor swimming pool.

advantages of being part of the military. A job in the military offers you a steady and reliable source of pay. You will be given free training in a specific job. You will enjoy a very special friendship with your fellow soldiers, who share your commitment to serving your country. On-base housing will be offered, as well as discounted groceries and medical services. There are other benefits, too. You may earn college tuition aid or assistance in buying a home once you have served the required time in one of the armed services. And, of course, you will more than likely have many chances to travel across the country and worldwide.

But a military life is not for everyone. A job in the military is in many ways unlike other jobs outside the military. Once you enlist, you are obliged, by law, to commit yourself to a specific term of military service. You cannot decide, as you might after accepting a civilian (or nonmilitary) job, that you do not like the military after all and simply quit. This is not allowed. The rules in the military can be very restrictive, and personal freedom is minimal. The training can be very difficult. The loss of independence can be very challenging. You must do as you are told, move from place to place as you are ordered, and salute and respect those who hold ranks above you, no matter how much you dislike them and want to refuse what they demand. Discipline and obedience are key factors in functioning successfully in any of the military services.

In times of war, you might have to face combat. Ask yourself if you are willing to do this. You might be asked to kill another human being and face the possibility of your own

Learning to protect and defend yourself in a hostile situation—such as hand-to-hand combat—is part of the military training for these marine recruits.

death or serious bodily harm. On the other hand, if you decide to join the military, you will be given a chance to learn self-discipline as well as leadership and vocational skills, things that can greatly advance you even after you have served your time and returned to civilian life.

Joining the Reserves

As mentioned earlier, there is another option when considering enlistment in the armed forces. You could join the reserves.

This means that you can gain the training and some of the benefits of a military career but still spend most of your time as a civilian.

Each branch of military service has a reserve unit. A reserve unit often requires only short-term commitments during the course of each year that you are a member. You might have training sessions over the weekend or will be required on occasion to spend a few weeks for special training. In an emergency, you might be called up for longer periods of time. This could involve either national emergencies or combat overseas. Joining the reserves does not mean that you won't be sent to war. Indeed, reserve units have shouldered a heavy portion of the burden in the war in Iraq. If you are interested in serving your country in a military capacity, however, but are not sure about making the military a full-time career, the reserves might be the perfect solution for you.

Requirements to Join the Military

To join any of the military services, you must be at least eighteen years old. Only if you have a permission slip signed by a parent or guardian can you join at age seventeen. You must be in good physical condition, as basic training (as well as your time in the service) will be very physically demanding. You should have a high school education. If not, you need to at least have a GED (General Education Development certificate). U.S. citizenship, or a legal permanent resident alien status, is also required.

Just remember that, as in any decision, it is best to ask as many questions as you can, to think about all your options, and

The desire to serve one's country is often inspired by family members who have been active in the military and who have fought for the United States in previous conflicts.

come to a logical and well-informed decision before signing your name to any papers. If a military career sounds like something you truly would like to do, take the next step necessary to make that happen. You have the advantage of having seen what military life can be like—its joys, hardships, privileges, and responsibilities—because you have already grown up in a military family.

Myths and Facts

 Children who grow up in military families are brats.

Fact: ➡ It is true that children who grow up in military families are often referred to as "military brats," but this term is more often used by those teens themselves than by civilian teens. In other words, it is a term that many teens in military families use to refer to themselves, almost as if it were a special club to belong to. The term has been used to express that children of military families often have experiences that are very different from children of nonmilitary families. Military children move around a lot, most make new friends every couple of years, and they must endure having their military parent leave the family for long periods of time. Embrace the term and use it proudly.

 Military housing is very bad. **Fact:** ➡ In recent years, houses on military bases have been renovated and improved, and new apartments and homes have been built. Also, the military offers families stipends (extra cash) to help them pay for housing in civilian neighborhoods off base. Houses and apartments, both on and off base, are similar to those in an average suburban neighborhood.

Joining the military is an easy way to get a free education.

Fact: ➡ Although you can gain college financial assistance by serving your time in the military, there are some drawbacks. First, most soldiers do not have the time or energy to take college classes until after they have completed their military service. Second, the money that the government offers does not always cover the full cost of tuition, books, and housing, so you will probably have to have a part-time job while attending school. Also, if you enlist only as a way to have college paid for, you may be caught off guard if war breaks out and you are obliged to head off to combat duty. Make sure you want to join and serve in the military for its own sake, not only as a stepping-stone to something else.

Glossary

anxiety A feeling of concern or nervousness about some past, current, or future event.

argumentation An attempt to convince someone else of a belief or idea you hold.

attitude A way of thinking, behaving, or feeling.

commitment The act of binding or dedicating yourself to a course of action.

cope To successfully deal with something difficult.

deployment In the military, receiving orders to be transported to another location without the family coming along.

military base An armed forces facility that includes places where soldiers work and live.

orders In the military, this is a formal written statement telling a soldier what his or her next job, assignment, or mission will be, as well as where he or she will need to travel to perform it.

Pentagon A five-sided building outside of Washington, D.C., where the U.S. Department of Defense is housed.

reminisce To recall or to remember fondly.

secretary of defense The person in charge of the Department of Defense who consults and advises the U.S. president on defense- and military-related issues and sets into motion the president's requests for military action.

symptoms Signs of physical , emotional, or psychological illness
or disease.

text messaging Sending instantaneous written messages via
cell phone or computer.

veteran Someone who has served in the military but is now
no longer a soldier; a former soldier who has re-entered
civilian life.

Department of Defense
1400 Defense Pentagon
Washington, DC 20301-1400
Web site: http://www.defenselink.mil
 The mission of the Department of Defense is to provide the
 military forces needed to deter war and protect the security
 of our country. The department's headquarters is at the
 Pentagon located outside of Washington, D.C. It is here
 that the secretary of defense directs the actions of the
 military through the orders of the president.

Department of National Defence
General Inquiries, Assistant Deputy Minister
 (Public Affairs)
National Defence Headquarters, Major-General George
 R. Pearkes Building
101 Colonel By Drive
Ottawa, ON, K1A 0K2
Canada
(613) 995-2534
(800) 467-9877
Web site: http://www.forces.gc.ca/site/home-accueil-eng.asp
 Canadian Forces members are proud to serve Canada by
 defending its values, interests, and sovereignty at home

and abroad. Canadian Forces personnel belong to air, land, sea, and special operations components.

Force Health Protection and Readiness (FHPR)
Skyline 4, Suite 901
5113 Leesburg Pike
Falls Church, VA 22401
Web site: http://fhp.osd.mil/index.jsp

The purpose of the FHPR is to enhance communication regarding the health of service members and their families. The site provides information to safeguard the health and well-being of service members and their families, promote and sustain a healthy and fit force, prevent injuries and illness and protect the force from health hazards, and sustain world-class medical and rehabilitative care to the sick and injured anywhere in the world.

Military Health System (MHS)
The Pentagon
Washington, DC 20301-1200
Web site: http://www.mhs.osd.mil

The MHS is prepared to respond anytime, anywhere with comprehensive medical capability to military operations, natural disasters, and humanitarian crises around the globe, and to ensure delivery of world-class health care to all Department of Defense service members, retirees, and their families. The MHS promotes a fit, healthy, and protected force by reducing non-combat losses, optimizing healthy behavior and physical performance, and providing casualty care. This organization combines the work of medical educators, medical researchers, and health-care providers who come from the medical departments of the U.S. Army, Navy, Marine Corps, Air Force, and Coast Guard.

National Military Family Association, Inc. (NMFA)
2500 Van Dorn Street, Suite 102
Alexandria, VA 22302-1601
(800) 260-0218
Web site: http://www.nmfa.org/site/PageServer
   The NMFA educates military families concerning the rights, benefits, and services available to them, and informs them regarding the issues that affect their lives. It also promotes and protects the interests of military families by influencing the development and implementation of legislation and policies affecting them.

Scholarships for Military Children
Fisher Hose Foundation
1401 Rockville Pike, Suite 600
Rockville, MD 20852
Web site: http://www.militaryscholar.org
   The Scholarships for Military Children program was created in recognition of the contributions of military families to the readiness of the fighting force and to celebrate the role of the commissary in the military family community.

U.S. Department of Veteran Affairs (VA)
810 Vermont Avenue NW
Washington, DC 20420
Web site: http://www.va.gov

The VA's goal is to provide excellence in patient care and veterans' benefits. The department's employees are dedicated and committed to helping veterans get the services they have earned.

Web Sites

Due to the changing nature of Internet links, Rosen Publishing has developed an online list of Web sites related to the subject of this book. This site is updated regularly. Please use this link to access this list:

http://www.rosenlinks.com/faq/mili

For Further Reading

Andrews, Beth, and Hawley Wright. *I Miss You! A Military Kid's Book About Deployment*. Amherst, NY: Prometheus Books, 2007.

Armstrong, Keith, et al. *Courage After Fire: Coping Strategies for Troops Returning from Iraq and Afghanistan and Their Families*. Berkeley, CA: Ulysses Press, 2005.

Dumler, Elaine Gray. *I'm Already Home . . . Again: Keeping Your Family Close While on Assignment or Deployment*. Salem, OR: Frankly Speaking, 2006.

Garrett, Sheryl, and Sue Hoppin. *A Family's Guide to the Military for Dummies*. Hoboken, NJ: For Dummies, 2008.

Gay, Kathlyn. *The Military and Teens: The Ultimate Teen Guide*. Lanham, MD: The Scarecrow Press, Inc., 2008.

Henderson, Kristin. *While They're at War: The True Story of American Families on the Home Front*. New York, NY: Mariner Books, 2006.

Pavlicin, Karen M. *Life After Deployment: Military Families Share Reunion Stories and Advice*. St. Paul, MN: Elva Resa Publishing, 2007.

Pavlicin, Karen M. *Surviving Deployment: A Guide for Military Families*. St. Paul, MN: Elva Resa Publishing, 2003.

Schindler, Michael J. R. *Operation Military Family: How to Strengthen Your Military Marriage and Save Your Family*. Lake Placid, NY: Aviva Publishing, 2007.

Index

About the Author

Joyce Hart is proud to say she is a "military brat." Her father was a career air force pilot who served for thirty years. In the course of her life in a military family, Hart attended seven schools before she graduated from high school. Some of the places she's lived in her youth include Boston, Massachusetts; Bermuda; Charleston, South Carolina; Washington, D.C.; and Orlando, Florida. The moving bug has affected much of Hart's adult life. In all, she has lived in thirteen different places. She is also the author of more than thirty nonfiction books for students.

Photo Credits

Cover © www.istockphoto.com/Yvonne Chamberlain; p. 5 © The Orange County Register/ZumaPress; p. 7 Don Emmert/AFP/Getty Images; p. 9 Brien Aho/U.S. Army; p. 11 Staff Sgt. Samuel Rogers/ U.S. Air Force; p. 18 © www.istockphoto.com/Sean Locke; p. 20 © www.istockphoto.com/Chris Schmidt; p. 24 Journalist 1st Class Mark Rankin/U.S. Navy; p. 26 Molly Hayden/U.S. Army Garrison-Hawaii Public Affairs; p. 28 Michael Morris/U.S. Army Garrison Vincenza, Italy; p. 30 © www.istockphoto.com/Sherly Griffin; p. 32 Staff Sgt. Leigh Bellinger/U.S. Air Force; p. 35 Sandy Huffaker/Getty Images; p. 36 © AP Images; p. 38 © www.istockphoto.com/Quavondo Nguyen; p. 41 Staff Sgt. A. C. Eggman/U.S. Air Force; p. 45 Mass Communication Specialist Seaman Patrick Grieco/U.S. Navy; p. 48 © Ed Murray/Star Ledger/Corbis; p. 49 Photographer's Mate 1st Class Michael Worner/ U.S. Navy; p. 51 Air Force Staff Sgt. Stacy Pearsall/U.S. Army; p. 53 © Michael Macor/San Francisco Chronicle/Corbis.

Designer: Nicole Russo; Photo Researcher: Amy Feinberg